Prophetic Power

Understanding the Prophetic Ministry

Kervin J. Smith

PNEUMA LIFE

PUBLISHING

Prophetic Power

Kervin J. Smith

Unless otherwise noted, Scripture quotations are taken from the *King James Version* of the Holy Bible. Scripture quotations marked NIV are taken from the *New International Version.* Copyright 1973, 1978, 1984, International Bible Society.

Printed in the United States of America
ISBN: 1-56229-471-7

Pneuma Life Publishing
P.O. Box 10612
Bakersfield, CA 93389-0612
(805) 324-1741

Contents

Acknowledgments
Dedication

Acknowledgments

Bishop Wilbert S. McKinley and Lady McKinley

Bishop Milton Perry

Christina Thompson

Fenton Rhaney

Janette Jones

Howard Winslow and Lynn Lovejoy

Virginia Parks

Dedication

To my parents, Joseph and Jean Smith, the greatest parents in the world.

Chapter 1

Prophetic Purpose

God is raising up an army of prophets who are proclaiming His Word throughout the world. How can you tell? Just look around you. Psychic networks, hotlines, and information are multiplying rapidly. Like rabbits, they quickly reproduce.

Sin pervades our nation. Our culture more readily embraces a life-style of sin than one of righteousness. Rebellion runs rampant. Our youth are on an all-time rebellious high. Their clothing, music, and attitudes shout, "Rebel!"

The Church suffers from a lack of respect. Clergy are killed inside their buildings. Hoodlums rob churches in the middle of the day. America is supposedly enjoying a time of "peace." Some peace.

These signs indicate something significant is happening in the kingdom of God. When God begins to usher in a new move of His Spirit, wickedness increases.

God is bringing His people into a new era, causing them to become the Prophetic Church. All across the world, prophets are emerging as spokesmen to nations. God has a word for the world, and He speaks it through His designated, commissioned mouthpiece: the prophet.

Despite this, many believers have never met a prophet of God. If you met one, you wouldn't necessarily recognize him or her (prophetess). We don't wear special clergy garments like pastors or bishops. We don't carry, nor do we need, special aids such as crystal balls, ouija boards, or tarot cards. Psychics need these items because they do not operate by the Holy Ghost, who resides within the born again prophet. Prophets are just ordinary believers who have been given the extraordinary task to echo God's Word.

When people meet me for the first time, they usually have many questions:

"What is a prophet?"

"How did you know that about me?"

"Does God speak to you in a voice, by pictures, or what?"

"Is it weird knowing things about people you never met?"

"Can you tell me about . . . ?"

Their curiosity is understandable. Whenever we encounter something new and different, we want to examine it from all angles. That's just human nature. I never get offended. As a matter of fact, I'm honored to be called and used by God in the prophetic ministry. I enjoy helping people to better understand my office.

Other people are quite knowledgeable about the prophetic ministry and the office of the prophet. Many of these individuals have read extensively on the ministry of the prophet. Others have been personally ministered to by a prophet. Another group has gained insight and understanding by tuning into various prophets on radio or TV.

Some have limited knowledge, having been exposed to a limited aspect of the prophetic ministry. Having some knowledge is better than none. Therefore, the Body of Christ, however, needs more in-depth teaching on the office and ministry of the prophet.

As the Body of Christ, we are now bringing to birth a new prophetic age. The church of the future will be the Prophetic Church. The Bible tells us that the prophetic office has been in effect since creation.

An Ever-Present Voice

Genesis, the book of beginnings, shows us God creating heaven and earth. In the first three verses of the book we see the triune God: God the Father (or Creator), God the Son, and God the Spirit.

God the Father is visible in Genesis 1:1, which reads, "In the beginning God created the heaven and the earth." A father is a life-giver who has the life-giving seed in His loins. As such He is a creator.

God the Father impregnated the heavens and earth with His life-giving seed. That seed produced everything we see in the world today. God rested on the seventh day because He completed His procreative purpose.

God the Son also spoke in creation. "And God said, Let there be light: and there was light" (Genesis 1:3). Jesus is the Word of God. Jesus also said, "I am the light of the world" (John 8:12). The Son spoke creation into existence. In the same way that He had power on earth to lay down His life and take it up, He also had power in the beginning.

God the Holy Spirit "moved upon the face of the waters" (Genesis 1:2).

The apostle John also verified that the triune God was at the helm of creation.

In the beginning was the Word, and the Word was with God, and the Word was God. The same was in the beginning with God. All things were made by him; and without him was not any thing made that was made. In him was life; and the life was the light of men (John 1:1-4).

That which was from the beginning, which we have heard, which we have seen with our eyes, which we have looked upon, and our hands have handled, of the Word of life; (For the life was manifested, and we have seen it, and bear witness, and shew unto you that eternal life, which was with the Father, and was manifested unto us;) (1 John 1:1,2).

If you examine these passages closely, you'll see the prophetic was an ever-present voice. Scripture says

God has "spoken by the mouth of all his holy prophets since the world began" (Acts 3:21).

The "word of the Lord" is a term frequently used in Scripture to denote a prophetic utterance. Genesis 1:3 contains the very first recorded incidence of prophecy in Scripture: "And God said." What did God say? "Let there be light."

How do we know God was prophesying? Scripture says, ". . . for the testimony of Jesus is the spirit of prophecy" (Revelation 19:10). God was speaking about His Son and testifying to His existence.

They Were Prophets Too

If I asked you to name several Old Testament prophets, you would probably mention Isaiah, Jeremiah, or Samuel. Those who have books of the Bible that bear their name are obvious choices. You might also think of those who had powerful, miraculous ministries such as Elijah or Elisha. Scripture tells us that other men were also considered prophets by God.

> Therefore also said the wisdom of God, I will send them prophets and apostles, and some of them they shall slay and persecute: That the blood of all the prophets, which was shed from the foundation of the world, may be required of this generation; From the blood of Abel unto the blood of Zecharias, which perished between the altar and the temple: verily I say unto you, It shall be required of this generation (Luke 11:49-51).

Luke indicates that Abel was a prophet. He is not seen prophesying in Scripture —probably because he was killed before his ministry manifested. Cain killed his brother out of jealousy over his brother's obedience to God in giving.

Your seed will attract attack. When you give offerings, you send a signal to the enemy that you possess money but it does not possess you. You become a thorn in the flesh to believers who do not exercise the faith to give.

Satan always tries to quiet the voice of the Lord. He often uses those who are close to God's prophets to do the killing. Cain killed Abel. Jesus was betrayed by Judas, a handpicked apostle of the Son of God.

Zacharias died at the hands of those who opposed his message of repentance.

And they left the house of the Lord God of their fathers, and served groves and idols: and wrath came upon Judah and Jerusalem for this their trespass. Yet he sent prophets to them, to bring them again unto the Lord; and they testified against them: but they would not give ear.

And the Spirit of God came upon Zechariah the son of Jehoiada the priest, which stood above the people, and said unto them, Thus saith God, Why transgress ye the commandments of the Lord, that ye cannot prosper? because ye have forsaken the Lord, he hath also forsaken you.

And they conspired against him, and stoned him with stones at the commandment of the king in the court of the house of the Lord. Thus Joash the king remembered not the kindness which Jehoiaha his father had done to him, but slew his son. And when he died, he said, The Lord look upon it, and require it (2 Chronicles 24:18-22).

Abraham was another prophet of old. Abraham? Yes, the father of faith was also a prophet. God revealed this to King Abimelech of Gerar in a dream after he took Sarah.

> But Abimelech had not come near her: and he said, Lord wilt thou slay also a righteous nation? Said he not unto me, She is my sister? and she, even she herself said, He is my brother: in the integrity of my heart and innocency of my hands have I done this.

> And God said unto him [Abimelech] in a dream, Yea, I know that thou didst this in the integrity of thy heart; for I also withheld thee from sinning against me: therefore suffered I thee not to touch her.

> Now therefore restore the man his wife; for he is a prophet, and he shall pray for thee, and thou shalt live: and if thou restore her not, know thou that thou shalt surely die, thou, and all that are thine (Genesis 20:4-7).

These examples prove that the prophetic ministry is rooted in the very fiber of the creation and in God's created showplace: the earth.

A Ministry for Today

According to Scripture the prophet should be an integral part of the New Testament church. I say *should* and not *is* because many churches still shun the ministry of the prophet. They welcome the pastor, evangelist, and teacher, but they close the door of the church when the prophet stops by. Their reluctance to receive this ministry gift doesn't change God's plans and purposes for the prophet, however.

> And God hath set some in the church, first apostles, secondarily prophets, thirdly teachers, after that miracles, then gifts of healings, helps, governments, diversities of tongues (1 Corinthians 12:28).

> And he gave some, apostles; and some, prophets; and some, evangelists; and some, pastors and teachers; For the perfecting of the saints, for the work of the ministry, for the edifying of the body of Christ: Till we all come in the unity of the faith, and of the knowledge of the Son of God, unto a perfect man, unto the measure of the stature of the fulness of Christ (Ephesians 4:11-13).

It is clear from the apostle Paul's teaching that prophets are indispensable. *Webster's Dictionary* defines indispensable as "absolutely necessary." Need I say more?

> For as the body is one, and hath many members, and all the members of that one body, being many, are one body: so also is Christ. For by one Spirit are we all baptized into one body, whether we be Jews or Gentiles, whether we be bond or free; and have been all made to drink into one Spirit. For the body is not one member, but many.

> If the foot shall say, Because I am not the hand, I am not of the body; is it therefore not of the body? And if the ear shall say, Because I am not the eye, I am not of the body; is it therefore not of the body? If the whole body were an eye, where were the hearing? If the whole were hearing, where were the smelling? But now hath God set the members every one of them in the body, as it hath pleased him (1 Corinthians 12:12-18).

God is the Head of the Body of Christ, and He sets each member in place as He desires. The same God who created Adam and said, "It is good," also created the Church and said, "It is good." Good becomes operative when everyone and everything is flowing in divine order, according to God's designated plans.

Pastors, beware! When you shut the door in the face of the prophet, you bar Jesus Christ the Prophet from your midst. Understanding that offending a prophet was a serious charge, even Abimelech obeyed the word of the Lord.

In this hour, God calls for the shepherds to embrace the prophet. He calls for a cooperative spirit exemplified by a close working relationship in which the pastor as head of the local assembly serves as overseer to the prophet but not as lord. He calls for prophets to submit to local leadership.

Prophet of God, listen to me. It is not your job to go into a local church and tear down the head of that assembly. It is not our role as prophets to lambast the pastor in front of his congregation and try to make it look good by adding a "thus saith the Lord" to validate the venomous garbage that some "prophesy." It is not your job to lord it over the pastor.

In my years in prophetic ministry, I have learned that the pastor-prophet relationship can be an equally yoked one that is mutually satisfying as long as each operates in divine order with the pastor as head and the prophet as God's mouthpiece.

Now ye are the body of Christ, and members in particular. And God hath set some in the church, first apostles, secondarily prophets, thirdly teachers, after that miracles, then gifts of healings, helps, governments, diversities of tongues (1 Corinthians 12:27,28).

God wants all of us working together and fulfilling our calling so that He might be glorified in our midst.

Who, Me? Misunderstood?

Have you ever had the feeling that no matter what you say or do, people misunderstand you? It happens all the time to the prophet. The prophetic ministry has been misrepresented and misunderstood.

The many aspects of the prophetic mantle make it easy for the prophet to be placed in the realm of an evangelist and never be accepted as a prophet. In fact, many prophets did not even use the title "Prophet" when they traveled years ago. Instead, they called themselves "Brother," "Elder," "Minister," and anything else that distanced them from the easily misunderstood calling upon their lives.

Because of the special and unique functions that accompany the office of the prophet, many of the visitations that come to the local church are aborted. New expressions of the Spirit of God are denied entrance by an invisible, yet real, "do not enter" sign. The fire of God to purify, equip, and empower the church is often quenched before the flames of revival and restoration can engulf believers. This must change.

Cost of the Prophetic Call

Jesus Christ wants to speak to His Body. He yearns to bring a fresh word to replace old waves of God that are still trying to stay afloat in some assemblies. His mouthpiece is the prophet. God has entrusted the prophet with His most precious secrets.

"Surely the Lord God will do nothing, but he revealeth his secret unto his servants the prophets" (Amos 3:7). God may reveal His secrets to the prophet, but man does not always celebrate him. The Bible clearly shows the persecution and suffering prophets have endured for the name of the Lord. Some have died as they walked in obedience to their call.

Satanic opposition is fierce. Satan would love to rid the land of God's prophets, but what would that prove? God would just raise up another — probably more radical — bunch of prophets and send them straight into the enemy's camp!

Prophets battle mockery, slander, and witchcraft. Isn't it odd that the Church won't celebrate the prophet, but the world celebrates the psychic? The world runs to the psychic with money in hand, looking for a word. The Church slams the door in the prophet's face and closes its fist. Or it hands the prophet a "love token" not fit to buy a decent meal.

Jealousy, envy, hate, and competition try to tear down the prophet. Now isn't that ridiculous? In Scripture the prophets of God fought the prophets of Baal — not each other. In fact, Elijah lamented that he was the only prophet in Israel, not knowing another 7,000 had not bowed their knee to Baal. That shows me the brother-hood of prophets was closely knit. They needed each other. The various schools of the prophets in Scripture also prove that the prophets bonded together and worked with — not against — each other.

But know this: the battlefield is the testing ground for those called into the prophetic ministry. Do not be deluded. A prophet will encounter many fiery furnace experiences. The purest gold emerges from the hottest flame. So it is with the prophet. Testing builds charac-ter.

> Behold, I have refined thee, but not with silver; I have chosen thee in the furnace of affliction (Isaiah 48:10).

> My brethren, count it all joy when ye fall into divers temp-tations; knowing this, that the trying of your faith worketh patience. But let patience have her perfect work, that ye may be perfect and entire, wanting nothing (James 1:2-4).

Prayer and the prophetic ministry go hand in hand. God will lead the prophet into hour after hour of prayer so that His servant can understand and relay the will of God. The call of the prophet mandates a life totally committed and consecrated to God.

Over time, the prophet will experience a metamor-phosis. His movement into deeper levels of God will change him. In the same way that a caterpillar changes into a butterfly, the prophet will emerge more vibrant when the transformation is complete. The resulting multifaceted mantle will bear witness to the diverse characteristics of God living in him.

Yes, the high call of prophetic ministry also has a high cost. Knowing the heart of God and having the privilege of conveying it to God's people, however, is a great reward.

Chapter 2

The Marks of a Prophet

When God desires to bring change, warning, judgment, and correction, He raises up a prophet. Winds of change blow as the prophet speaks life into valley after valley of dry bones. He steers them into God's chosen pathways of blessings. He awakens their desire for elevation in Christ. Often many treasures that God has for His people cannot be released unless a prophet opens the lid.

No two prophets will minister exactly alike. Scripture reveals a plethora of ways prophets ministered in the past. Prophets ministered to nations. They anointed new government leaders, especially kings. Prophets worked miracles, including raising the dead. Prophets served as statesmen or advisers to kings.

Today, prophets still play a vital role in national and international affairs. You may not know it, but prophets are providing God's directives to government leaders on every level. A prophet does not have to authenticate his ministry by saying, "Look, here I am in Washington, D.C., prophesying to the president." That's what a psychic would do because he or she wants to get the glory. The prophet is content to do his job and head toward the next assignment that God gives him.

Distinctive Characteristics

Although one prophet's ministry may differ from another's, some distinctive characteristics mark the prophet.

1. He is a loner. The prophetic call isolates the prophet. He often walks through the valley by himself. A prophet will not allow people to control his destiny. His actions cannot be constrained by diplomats in the world or in the Church. He does not want to be with the "in crowd." Actually, he can't be with the "in crowd" because his message usually rubs them the wrong way. While others applaud their efforts, the prophet stands alone and says, "Thus saith the Lord, 'Change your ways.'"

2. He is a spokesman. He is aware of the mandate that has been set forth by God and therefore speaks — even in the midst of opposition, strife, and confusion. He can't back down. He cannot allow himself to be bribed. If he does, he will step out of the will of God.

And Balak sent yet again princes, more, and more honourable than they. And they came to Balaam, and said to him, Thus saith Balak the son of Zippor, Let nothing, I pray thee, hinder thee from coming to me: For I will promote thee unto very great honour, and I will do whatsoever thou sayest unto me: come therefore, I pray thee, curse me this people (Numbers 22:15-17).

The Book of Numbers includes three chapters on Balaam. His story illustrates how God deals with anyone who attempts to speak for God but goes beyond God's message. His story also warns prophets not to accept bribes. Do not add or take away from that which God puts in your mouth to speak. Disobedience and presumption may cost you your life.

Balaam's disobedience nearly killed him. Balak sent messengers to Balaam requesting that Balaam curse the children of Israel. Why? Because "I wot that he whom thou blessest is blessed, and he whom thou cursest is cursed" (Numbers 22:6).

God told Balaam, "Thou shalt not go with them; thou shalt not curse the people: for they are blessed" (Numbers 22:12). After consulting God, Balaam declined to go. He told the messengers, who were princes of Moab, that God would not let him go.

To be fair to Balaam, he refused to go. Yet his words indicated his heart had begun to waver. "If Balak would give me his house full of silver and gold, I cannot go beyond the word of the Lord my God, to do less or more" (Numbers 22:18).

The temptation prompted him to promise to pray again to God for an answer. God granted permission for the double-minded prophet to go, but His anger burned against Balaam.

To bring the prophet to his senses, the angel of the Lord blocked Balaam's path three times. The stubborn, disobedient prophet could not see the heavenly messenger, but the ass that he was riding did. God opened the mouth of the animal to speak to the rebellious prophet.

> Then the Lord opened the eyes of Balaam, and he saw the angel of the Lord standing in the way, and his sword drawn in his hand: and he bowed down his head, and fell flat on his face.
>
> And the angel of the Lord said unto him, Wherefore hast thou smitten thine ass these three times? b ehold, I went out to withstand thee, because thy way is perverse before me: And the ass saw me, and turned from me these three times: unless she had turned from me, surely now also I had slain thee, and saved her alive.
>
> And Balaam said unto the angel of the Lord, I have sinned; for I knew not that thou stoodest in the way against me: now therefore, if it displease thee, I will get me back again.
>
> And the angel of the Lord said unto Balaam, Go with the men: but only the word that I shall speak unto thee, that thou shalt speak. So Balaam went with the princes of Balak (Numbers 22:31-35).

In the end, Balaam spoke only the oracles of God.

3. He is God's mediator. As such, he is given mysteries from God to minister to the hearts of hurting and needy individuals. A word from God let Samuel know that the donkey's of Saul's father had been found. God used that incident to lead Saul into a prophetic encounter regarding his destiny as Israel's first king.

4. He has an unusual demeanor. Because of the power of God resident in the prophet and the revealed things he receives, the prophet is known to have an unusual demeanor. He may be up one moment and down the next. Elijah proved this. After a successful confrontation with 450 prophets of Baal, Elijah ran for his life from Jezebel. His strength, weakness, and fear were demonstrated in successive order.

5. He knows that God is backing him. God leads the prophet down some peculiar roads, but like Jeremiah found out, he must trust that God will protect his back. "And they shall fight against thee; but they shall not prevail against thee; for I am with thee, saith the Lord, to deliver thee" (Jeremiah 1:19).

6. He is a person of prayer and consecration. The prophet enters into prayer prepared to commune with God, listen to God, and fellowship with God. He awaits the message that God is stirring for that hour.

7. He is a person of character and integrity. A prophet still has the potential to sin and be swayed, just like any other human being. Integrity is so crucial for the prophet, however, that he should seek it relentlessly. Remember, the prophet speaks for God. If his life speaks louder than his ministry, people will erroneously blame God and not the prophet.

Prophet of God, gird up the loins of your mind and decide that integrity is your portion. Walk like the God you speak for. Do not let your mouth utter one thing and your body another. Willingly embrace the Word of God and walk by its mandates. Do not take short cuts to success.

8. He is aware of world events. A prophet must be knowledgeable. He is guided by the will of God to raise his voice and protest against social injustices. The prophets of God were radical. God used them like battering rams against walls of oppression and sin. They got involved in the political structures of their day to bring the word of the Lord to the God's people and the heathen nations.

Stepping Stones to Ministry

Each prophet must follow nine steps in his ministry.

1. Be godly. "So God created man in his own image, in the image of God created he him; male and female created he them" (Genesis 1:27).

2. Embrace humility. "By humility and the fear of the Lord are riches, and honour, and life" (Proverbs 22:4).

3. Pray. "Pray without ceasing" (1 Thessalonians 5:17).

4. Embrace the call. "Before I formed thee in the belly I knew thee; and before thou cameth forth out of the womb I sanctified thee, and I ordained thee a prophet unto the nations" (Jeremiah 1:5).

5. Be careful. "This is a faithful saying, and these things I will that thou affirm constantly, that they which have believed in God might be careful to maintain good works" (Titus 3:8).

6. Be diligent. "The hand of the diligent shall bear rule: but the slothful shall be under tribute" (Proverbs 12:24).

7. Be orderly. "Let all things be done decently and in order" (1 Corinthians 14:40).

8. Control yourself. "Be self-controlled and alert. Your enemy the devil prowls around like a roaring lion looking for someone to devour" (1 Peter 5:8, NIV).

9. Embrace purity. "Flee fornication. Every sin that a man doeth is without the body; but he that committeth fornication sinneth against his own body" (1 Corinthians 6:18).

By carefully cultivating these qualities in your life, you will walk in integrity — a necessary prerequisite for others to receive you, your ministry, and your message.

Chapter 3

The Office of a Prophet

Isaiah perceived the will of God for his life in a vision and embraced the office of the prophet.

And he laid it upon my mouth, and said, Lo, this hath touched thy lips; and thine iniquity is taken away, and thy sin purged.

Also I heard the voice of the Lord, saying, Whom shall I send, and who will go for us? Then said I, Here am I; send me (Isaiah 6:7,8).

What is a Prophet?

A prophet is a person whom God has uniquely equipped to speak for Him. The prophet is the mouthpiece of God.

Then the Lord put forth his hand, and touched my mouth. And the Lord said unto me, Behold I have put my words in thy mouth (Jeremiah 1:9).

With the word of the Lord, he or she (prophetess) speaks the oracles of God — the very words God has ordained to be uttered for a given time, season, or people.

The prophet receives direct divine revelation from God and speaks the message God has given. Like an echo, he repeats what he has heard and how he heard it. His is called to deliver the message as he received it to the people for which it was sent.

> God, who at sundry times and in divers manners spake in time past unto the fathers by the prophets (Hebrews 1:1).

God speaks to the prophet. The prophet speaks to the people. Like a ready-to-eat meal, the prophet adds nothing to the message. Nor does he hold anything back. His sole responsibility is to deliver the message as God wants it spoken. In so doing, the prophet is given the awesome task to reprimand, dissuade, intervene, teach, and advise.

As messengers of God, prophets are sent to speak a word that revolutionizes people's lives. Prophets are agents of transformation. God sends prophets to bring transformation on every level: spiritually, physically, economically, politically, and socially.

The Bible tells us that true prophets were men that only God had sent. They did not receive or act on instructions from man!

> The prophet which prophesieth of peace, when the word of the prophet shall come to pass, then shall the prophet

be known, that the Lord hath truly sent him (Jeremiah 28:9).

And the Lord took me as I followed the flock, and the Lord said unto me, Go, prophesy unto my people Israel (Amos 7:15).

The Roll Call of the Prophets

Most of our Bible heros were prophets and prophetesses. Well-known prophets with established, public ministries included the following individuals:

The Early Group
Moses in Egypt
Samuel in Israel
Elijah in Israel
Elisha in Israel
Joel in Jerusalem
Jonah in Israel

The Eighth Century Group
Amos in Israel
Hosea in Israel
Isaiah in Jerusalem
Micah in Jerusalem

The Seventh Century Group
Zephaniah in Jerusalem
Jeremiah in Jerusalem and Egypt
Nahum in Jerusalem
Habakkuk in Jerusalem

The Exilic Group
Obadiah in Jerusalem or Babylon
Ezekiel in Babylon
Daniel in Babylon

The Post-Exilic Group
Haggai in Jerusalem
Zechariah in Jerusalem
Malachi in Jerusalem

Old Testament Prophetesses
Deborah
Huldah

Pre-New Testament Church
John the Baptist
Zacharias
Jesus

New Testament Church
Agabus
Barnabus
Simeon
Lucius of Cyrene
Judas
Silas

The Prophet's Mantle

Foretelling is one dimension of the prophetic ministry. Foretelling involves the disclosure of future events. People often think that this is all a prophet does: he tells you what will happen. You must never restrict prophecy to the foretelling of the future, however. If you do, you handcuff the ministry and the man.

Prophets also speak of current events. Scripture shows us how they led Israel into the will and plan of God. They often beseeched Israel to fulfill its mandate to serve the living God who raised them up from one man to a nation of millions.

Some people would love to be prophets. Unless you are called, however, you will not walk the prophetic path. Only the Lord handpicks and chooses His prophets without the awareness, permission, or direction of other individuals.

Amos quickly admitted that he never asked to be a prophet. Nor was he in line to walk in that calling; he was not the son of a prophet. He was a herdsman. He liked his job and was not seeking elevation to the prophetic office.

God had other plans, however. God literally uprooted Amos from his comfortable way of life and thrust upon him the prophetic mantle and burden. This country boy was not trained by the school of the prophets, nor did he attend any specialized or formal ministerial courses. After calling him, God trained and developed Amos in prophetic ministry.

> Then answered Amos, and said to Amaziah, I was no prophet, neither was I a prophet's son; but I was an herdman, and a gatherer of sycomore fruit: And the Lord took me as I followed the flock, and the Lord said unto me, Go, prophesy unto my people Israel (Amos 7:14,15).

Amos shows how God can take a person who is uneducated and give him the grace, ability, and mind of a professor. Most of the people in Amos' day thought he was a literary genius. He prophesied as a contemporary of Hosea, Micah, Isaiah, and Jonah.

Like Amos, Isaiah also was not a prophet. Yet he heard the voice of God, willingly answered that call to ministry, and knew he would emerge as a spokesman for Jehovah.

God burned a message into Micah's heart and endowed him with power to deliver it.

Jeremiah, a quiet young man, lacked purpose in the natural. He had no clue that from his birth God had clothed him with a special responsibility. He had to be set apart and placed into an occupation from which he would never turn. He was born to prophesy to his people and save the nation.

Sometimes prophets don't even know that they are called until they have a divine encounter. God told Jeremiah that he was predestined to be a messenger of God.

Before I formed thee in the belly I knew thee; and before thou cameth forth out of the womb I sanctified thee, and I ordained thee a prophet unto the nations (Jeremiah 1:5).

God's messengers are also men of authority. Their very words were — and are —God-given. God speaks to their minds and spirits so they can articulate through their lips. Like an expectant mother, they carry, protect, and give birth to the seed in due season.

I will raise them up a Prophet from among their brethren, like unto thee, and will put my words in his mouth; and he shall speak unto them all that I shall command him (Deuteronomy 18:18).

In Scripture, the language of prophecy differed from one prophet's administration of his office to another. Prophetic messages were delivered in parables, allegories, similes, riddles, and symbolism. God chose the vehicle of expression so the recipient would understand the message.

When I minister to people, sometimes they act like they don't know what I'm talking about — especially when I hit on areas of sin. Their expression says, "Prophet, you have missed it." I didn't miss it. They know exactly what God is saying. They are just dumbfounded that He revealed it to me! Everything hidden shall be revealed. That's the promise of God.

When the prophet speaks, he often says, "I will do this" or "I have begun to . . ." He articulates the word of the Lord in this manner, speaking personally for God. "I" refers to God in his message. "And thou shalt know that I am the Lord" (1 Kings 20:13). "Thus saith the Lord, Ye have forsaken me" (2 Chronicles 12:5).

Prophetic revelation was delivered orally. Isaiah, Jeremiah, and Daniel, however, also delivered messages in writing.

The Prophet and the Seer

In the Old Testament, prophets were also known as seers.

(Beforetime in Israel, when a man went to inquire of God, thus he spake, Come, and let us go to the seer: for he that is now called a Prophet was beforetime called a Seer) (1 Samuel 9:9).

The Hebrew words for prophets are *roeh* and *hazeh.* They are derived from *raah* and *hazah,* which mean "to see. "Actually, the meaning is "one who sees," or "seer."

Saul and his servant called the prophet Samuel the seer when they sought him for direction. They inquired, "Is the seer here?" (1 Samuel 9:11).

The Israelites recognized the seer's ministry as a valuable resource. A person would bring a gift to the seer when seeking direction. The tradition was so entrenched in the culture that Saul was distressed that he did not have anything to give to Samuel.

At the time, Saul was searching for his father's lost donkeys. After a futile search, Saul wanted to give up. His wise servant, however, suggested they go ask the seer. They took a gift to the seer, not as a payment but to honor the man of God.

Samuel had a well-established and well-respected ministry. Saul's servant described him as "an honourable man; all that he saith cometh surely to pass" (1 Samuel 9:6).

The people recognized Samuel as both a seer and a prophet. "And all Israel from Dan even to Beer-sheba knew that Samuel was established to be a prophet of the Lord" (1 Samuel 3:20).

Saul met Samuel in the city gate and asked him the whereabouts of the seer. He stood in the very presence of the man he needed but didn't know it. Like many today, he could not recognize the anointed man of God sent to bring change in his life.

Then Saul drew near to Samuel in the gate, and said, Tell me, I pray thee, where the seer's house is.

And Samuel answered Saul, and said, I am the seer: go up before me unto the high place; for ye shall eat with me to day, and to morrow I will let thee go, and will tell thee all that is in thine heart (1 Samuel 9:18,19).

God had sent Samuel to anoint Saul as king. While Saul was seeking one thing from the seer, he received something altogether different.

It is the same today. People come to the prophet with preconceived ideas of what they want to hear. They might even whisper in the prophet's ear, "This seed is for my son." "This seed is for my household." Many times God honors that. Other times, the prophet is not allowed to touch those areas because God has a higher order.

It is important to receive the prophetic message with the right heart and attitude. If God doesn't speak to you what you think He should, don't get mad. Remember, He's God.

Saul's encounter with the seer dramatically changed the course of his life. It brought transformation. It brought deliverance from mediocrity. It brought purpose.

These are also the hallmarks of the prophet's ministry. The role of the seer and its related Hebrew word, *roeh*, eventually emerged as *nabhi* or prophet.

Nabhi comes from the word *nabha*, which is an emotional fervor that bubbles within the prophet. Sometimes the prophet is overcome with an emotion akin to ecstasy.

As defined "to see," *roeh* and *hozeh* show the revelational perspective of the prophet. They heard from God and discerned His will. The *nabhi*, conversely, spoke forth information given during time of revelation. Think of it this way. The *roeh-hozeh* tells us about the reception of the messenger; the *nabhi* gives forth his message.

A Matter of Distinctions

The *roeh-hozeh* worked alone. The *nabhi* worked in groups. The *roeh-hozeh* waited for consultation, for people to seek him out. Not so with the *nabhi*. In some cases, the *roeh*, "seer" and the *hozeh* became the "prophet." The distinctions are sometimes blurred, but the fact remains that God desires to speak to His people. The seer and the prophet are vehicles through which God can speak.

An example of the *nabhi* in action can be found in Exodus 7. Moses felt dejected when God opened his eyes to the role of the *nabhi*.

And the Lord said unto Moses, See I have made thee a god to Pharaoh: and Aaron thy brother shall be thy prophet (Exodus 7:1).

Having been trained and educated among the leaders of Egypt, Moses was destined to be a great leader.

But he couldn't see beyond his speech impediment. He tried to use his natural limitations to short-circuit the work of God.

Doesn't that sound familiar? Christians are always telling God what they can't do.

God reminded Moses that He, "I am that I am," is the author and finisher of Moses' faith. God side-stepped Moses' excuses and let him know that Jehovah Jireh will provide the instructions. He appointed Aaron as Moses' spokesman.

> And thou shalt speak unto him, and put words in his mouth: and I will be with thy mouth, and with his mouth, and will teach you what ye shall do.
>
> And he shall be thy spokesman unto the people: and he shall be, even he shall be to thee instead of a mouth, and thou shalt be to him instead of God (Exodus 4:15,16).

True or False Prophet?

One of the marks of the latter days is the rise of false prophets. How can we know who is really prophesying the oracles of God?

> The Lord thy God will raise up unto thee a Prophet from the midst of thee, of thy brethren, like unto me; unto him ye shall hearken;
>
> According to all that thou desiredst of the Lord thy God in Horeb in the day of the assembly, saying, Let me not hear again the voice of the Lord my God, neither let me see this great fire any more, that I die not.

And the Lord said unto me, They have well spoken that which they have spoken. I will raise them up a Prophet from among their brethren, like unto thee, and will put my words in his mouth; and he shall speak unto them all that I shall command him.

And it shall come to pass, that whosoever will not hearken unto my words which he shall speak in my name, I will require it of him.

But the prophet, which shall presume to speak a word in my name, which I have not commanded him to speak, or that shall speak in the name of other gods, even that prophet shall die. And if thou say in thine heart, How shall we know the word which the Lord hath not spoken?

When a prophet speaketh in the name of the Lord, if the thing follow not, nor come to pass, that is the thing which the Lord hath not spoken, but the prophet hath spoken it presumptuously; thou shalt not be afraid of him (Deuteronomy 18:15-22).

Moses' exhortation to the nation provided two keys in understanding the prophetic ministry:

1. Not all who spoke in the name of the Lord were sent by God.

2. The prophetic ministry could be proven or tested.

If what the prophet prophesied came to pass, he was a true messenger of God. If the prophecy did not come to pass, he was a false prophet. The true prophet should be respected. The false prophet should be ignored.

A word of caution: just because the prophecies spoken over you have yet to manifest, do not assume the prophet was false. Remember, Isaiah prophesied about the virgin birth of Jesus 400 years before the word of the Lord came to pass.

The prophet speaks in the prophetic perfect. He sees that thing already accomplished. Sometimes it may take weeks, months, or even years for the word of the Lord to come to pass. But don't despair. Do not faint. The word of the Lord is sure. It will come to pass.

God will place His words in a man's mouth and activate him to speak words of life or death. Whatever the message, the true prophet will only speak what God instructs him to speak.

And the angel of the Lord said unto Balaam, Go with the men: but only the word that I speak unto thee, that thou shalt speak (Numbers 22:35).

The Word Will Correct

Like the written Word of God, the spoken prophetic word is a two-edged sword that both cuts and heals, often simultaneously. There have been times in history, however, where God was deliberately silent. When God began to speak again through His prophets, it brought fresh fire to Israel.

During King Manasseh's reign, prophecy was denied its proper expression. God used an invasion to unstop the prophetic flow.

The Greek scholar Herodotus tells us, "These marauders invaded the kingdom of the Medes in battle. They ruled over Asia 28 years. Assyria and Palestine were shaken by the invasion. Ruthless soldiers on horseback penetrated the hills of Judah. They viciously annihilated anything in their way and drank the blood of their victims, using skulls as drinking cups. If that was not bad enough, they also made clothing by searing together the scalps of their enemies."

Their reign of terror ignited a cry for the voice of the Lord. An alarm was sounded for a voice to come forth. That voice appeared in Zephaniah, who, along with Nahum and Habakkuk, were known as the three prophets of transition.

A prince and prophet, Zephaniah is the only prophet to trace his lineage over four generations: King Hezekiah, Amariah, Gedaliah, and Cushi. His ministry began with the reign of King Josiah, who came to the throne at the age of eight and reigned 31 years in Jerusalem.

A key adviser to the boy king, Zephaniah helped steer Josiah in the ways of the Lord. Zephaniah's role in the kingdom was essential because King Josiah came from a long line of spiritual dissenters.

Manasseh, his wicked grandfather, reintroduced idol worship in the temple of God. His sin brought the fiery judgment of God on Judah and Jerusalem. According to Scripture, Manasseh provoked God to anger, shed innocent blood, and even made Judah to sin (2 Kings 21:11-18).

Amon, Josiah's father, walked in Manasseh's footsteps. In his two-year reign, before he was murdered by his own servants, Amon, "did that which was evil in the sight of the Lord, as his father Manasseh did. And he walked in all the way that his father walked in, and served the idols that his father served, and worshipped them: And he forsook the Lord God of his fathers, and walked not in the way of the Lord (2 Kings 21:20-22).

Zephaniah's ministry bore fruit in King Josiah's life. Between the ages of 16 and 18, Josiah launched a spiritual reformation. He destroyed anything that was not of God. He ordered the graven images to be burned. "And he did that which was right in the sight of the Lord, and walked in all the way of David his father, and turned not aside to the right hand or to the left" (2 Kings 22:2). The corrective ministry of the prophet helped Josiah to be steadfast.

Chapter 4

The Function of a Prophet

The main function of every prophet is to receive revelation from God and to speak forth the word of the Lord. Why is God's prophetic word so important? Scripture tells us, "Surely the Lord God will do nothing, but he revealeth his secret unto his servants the prophets" (Amos 3:7).

The prophetic word is sent to provide revelation and cause people to respond. God often used the prophet as a vessel of repentance, showing God's mercy to His covenant people.

The prophet's ministry often produced reformation. Prophets were charged with reinforcing the need for repentance. They ministered directly to individuals, as well as entire nations. Prophets were also summoned by national leaders to give counsel and to speak a word of the Lord.

Go and cry in the ears of Jerusalem, saying, Thus saith the Lord; I remember thee, the kindness of thy youth, the love of thine espousals, when thou wentest after me in the wilderness, in a land that was not sown (Jeremiah 2:2).

A prophet's public ministry meets people where they live, work, and worship.

Stand in the gate of the Lord's house, and proclaim there this word, and say, Hear the word of the Lord, all ye of Judah, that enter in at these gates to worship the Lord (Jeremiah 7:2).

Thus said the Lord unto me; Go and stand in the gate of the children of the people, whereby the kings of Judah come in, and by the which they go out, and in all the gates of Jerusalem. And say unto them, Hear ye the word of the Lord, ye kings of Judah, and all Judah, and all the inhabitants of Jerusalem, that enter in by these gates (Jeremiah 17:19,20).

Each prophet was called during a time of intellectual, social, and political tension. Isaiah was called in "the year that King Uzziah died" (Isaiah 6:1). Micah came forth during a time of idolatry and immorality. Jeremiah prophesied during the period before the Babylonian exile.

Despite the different settings in which they ministered, each of these prophets were called. They gave up their careers, families, and plans for the future to embrace the call. Their willingness to speak boldly in the face of opposition, war, famine, and political upheaval set them apart from the false prophets of their day. The Spirit of the Lord led them, and they did mighty exploits in His name.

Jeremiah prophesied in public places. He preached and prophesied as people went about their daily tasks.

Daniel's ministry exemplified the role of the prophet as spokesman, teacher, and statesmen.

As an integral link in the fivefold ministry today, the prophet works alongside apostles, pastors, evangelists, and teachers to help build up the Body of Christ. Together, they comprise an awesome team equipped to build up, train, and maintain the Body of Christ.

God wants to speak to His Body. It is time for the Body of Christ to begin recognizing ordained prophets and to begin using them in their proper place in the Body.

> For as the body is one, and hath many members, and all the members of that one body, being many, are one body: so also is Christ. For by one Spirit are we all baptized into one body, whether we be Jews or Gentiles, whether we be bond or free; and have been all made to drink into one Spirit (1 Corinthians 12:12,13).

If one body part is out of place, the entire human body suffers. If the head aches, all the other parts of the body also are affected. So it is in the Body of Christ.

All parts of the fivefold ministry must work together, pulling for the common good of the entire Body of Christ. If one human body part is missing — suppose an arm — the other body parts must work harder.

The same principle applies in the kingdom of God. As long as prophets are not allowed to function, the

Body of Christ will not reach its maximum maturity or effectiveness. It is time for a change.

Chapter 5

Prophetic Prayer

Prayer is vital to the prophetic ministry. Prophets must consider prayer as their lifeline. Just as blood is essential to the life of the body, prayer is vital to the quality of the prophet's life and ministry.

Prayer, which in principal means to communicate with God, has no substitute. It is a mandate for the entire Body of Christ. For prophets and others alike, prayer allows us to enter into a personal relationship with God.

The prophet, in prayer, begins to develop a life devoted to God. In prayer God begins to mold, develop, and deal with His prophets. The prophet feels the weight of his ministry during prayer. He often feels the burdens, afflictions, weights, and pains of the people to whom he is called. How well Jeremiah knew and experienced this!

O Lord, thou knowest: remember me, and visit me, and revenge me of my persecutors; take me not away in thy longsuffering: know that for thy sake I have suffered rebuke.

Thy words were found, and I did eat them; and thy word was unto me the joy and rejoicing of mine heart: for I am called by thy name, O Lord God of hosts.

I sat not in the assembly of the mockers, nor rejoiced; I sat alone because of thy hand: for thou hast filled me with indignation. Why is my pain perpetual, and my wound incurable, which refuseth to be healed? wilt thou be altogether unto me as a liar, and as waters that fail? (Jeremiah 15:15-18).

Prayer is like oxygen to the prophetic ministry. In order for the prophet to breathe the "word of the Lord," he must learn how to enter into the presence of the Lord.

The prophet must become an expert at taking his petitions to God and sitting and listening attentively. As God gives the prophet a fresh word, often the prophet just listens. He is still before the Lord. On some occasions, even in Scripture, the Lord will instruct the prophet to write what "Thus saith the Lord."

And the Lord answered me, and said, Write the vision, and make it plain upon tables, that he may run that readeth it (Habakkuk 2:2).

In order to utter the oracles of God — a sure word that is fresh from the throne room of heaven — you must have a prayer life. There is no way around it. A prophet must develop a consistent habit of praying — daily!

Each person will have a particular way that he brings himself into the presence of God. There is no one prescribed way or set-in-stone time mandated by God to pray. Praise and worship will also be vital components of every prophet's prayer life.

The more you pray, the easier the prophetic will flow in your life. The more you pray, the easier it will be to hear the voice of God. Prayer makes you extremely keen and sensitive to the voice of the Lord. The prophet must understand that God is always speaking. We must learn to tune our spirit into the right frequency.

Isaiah, perhaps the greatest Old Testament prophet, knew how to enter the presence of Lord. He became an intimate lover of God. He knew how to bring forth praise and adoration unto God. And he did it unabashedly. He abandoned himself to knowing God intimately.

Often we become intimate with our spouses or develop a deep relationship with families and friends but are lukewarm toward God. God seeks intimacy with us. He wants you to know Him on a deeper level than ever before. Enter in. Be like Isaiah and know your God.

O Lord, thou art my God; I will exalt thee, I will praise thy name; for thou hast done wonderful things; thy counsels of old are faithfulness and truth.

For thou hast made of a city an heap; of a defenced city a ruin: a palace of strangers to be no city; it shall never be built.

Therefore shall the strong people glorify thee, the city of the terrible nations shall fear thee. For thou hast been a strength to the poor, a strength to the needy in his distress, a refuge from the storm, a shadow from the heat, when the blast of the terrible ones is as a storm against the wall.

Thou shalt bring down the noise of strangers, as the heat in a dry place; even the heat with the shadow of a cloud: the branch of the terrible ones shall be brought low.

And in this mountain shall the Lord of hosts make unto all people a feast of fat things, a feast of wines on the lees, of fat things full of marrow, of wines on the lees well refined.

And he will destroy in this mountain the face of the covering cast over all people, and the ve il that is spr ead over all nations. He will swallow up death in victory; and the Lord God will wipe away tears from off all faces; and the rebuke of his people shall he take away from off all the earth: for the Lord hath spoken it (Isaiah 25:1-8).

Intercessory Prayer

Prophets were, and are, among the greatest intercessors of the Body of Christ. They intercede, or petition God, on behalf of others. Afflicted by the people for whom he prayed, Jeremiah reminded God of his intercession for them: "Shall evil be recompensed for good? for they have digged a pit for my soul. Remember that I stood before thee to speak good for them, and to turn away thy wrath from them" (Jeremiah 18:20).

Scripture shows us a king and prophet in the temple crying out to God for a breakthrough. "And for this cause Hezekiah the king, and the prophet Isaiah the son of Amoz, prayed and cried to heaven" (2 Chronicles 32:20).

We also find a classic case of a prophet standing in the gap, crying out to God while interceding for the children of God. As Hezekiah and Isaiah cried out together to God, heaven shook. Things happen when the prophet prays. All throughout Scripture we see examples of mighty works resulting from a prophet's intercessory prayer.

Yes, there is power in praying for other people's circumstances and conditions. This power is awesome, inexplicable, and very real.

As an intercessory team, Hezekiah and Isaiah saw results. As they interceded, the Lord began to slay the Assyrian army.

During the period of the judges, another prophet interceded for God's people. At that time Israel had begun to worship graven images and practice idolatry. Because he had an intimate relationship with God, the prophet Samuel gathered the nation together and prayed to the Lord. In essence, this was corporate intercession.

And the children of Israel said to Samuel, Cease not to cry unto the Lord our God for us, that he will save us out of the hand of the Philistines. And Samuel took a sucking lamb, and offered it for a burnt offering wholly unto the Lord: and Samuel cried unto the Lord for Israel; and the Lord heard him.

And as Samuel was offering up the burnt offering, the Philistines drew near to battle against Israel: but the Lord thundered with a great thunder on that day upon the Philistines, and discomfited them; and they were smitten before Israel (1 Samuel 7:8-10).

The prophet has a twofold intercessory task:

1. He must call upon the Lord.

2. He must take petitions to God for the spiritual life of his people. The prophet must speak for the people to whom he belongs.

O Lord, though our iniquities testify against us, do thou it for thy name's sake: for our backslidings are many; we have sinned against thee.

O the hope of Israel, the savior thereof in time of trouble, why shouldest thou be as a stranger in the land, and as a wayfaring man that turneth aside to tarry for a night?

Why shouldest thou be as a man astonied, as a mighty man that cannot save? yet thou, O Lord, art in the midst of us, and we are called by thy name; leave us not (Jeremiah 14:7-9).

The person who walks in the prophetic must have a prayer life. When a word or oracle is needed for a special circumstance or situation, the prayerful prophet will be able to deliver a clear and fresh word of the Lord.

In those days was Hezekiah sick unto death. And the prophet Isaiah the son of Amoz came to him, and said unto him, Thus saith the Lord, Set thine house in order; for thou shalt die, and not live.

Then he turned his face to the wall, and prayed unto the Lord, saying, I beseech thee, O Lord, remember now how I have walked before thee in truth and with a perfect heart, and have done that which is good in thy sight. And Hezekiah wept sore.

And it came to pass, afore Isaiah was gone out into the middle court, that the word of the Lord came to him, saying . . . I will heal thee (2 Kings 20:1-5).

A Life of Fasting

The prophet will also be a person who fasts. He will be dedicated to going to God empty so that God will deposit something in him. Prophets know the tremendous benefits of fasting. Prayer and fasting go hand in hand. A wise prophet, therefore, will develop a well-rounded prayer and fasting life.

Prayer and fasting are power tools. They break up the hard places in a prophet's heart. They expose his failures and weaknesses. They strengthen him for the road. They help him to hear God more clearly. Even singers understand that an empty vessel often operates better!

Through fasting, the prophet begins to know God's ways and will become more sensitive to God. He will begin to develop a thirst for hearing the clarion call of the Lord. Anyone who wants to be used of God to the fullest extent will be a person who fasts and prays.

Fasting helps an individual to develop greater self-discipline, which is a key to walking in the fullness of God's Word, His anointing, and His presence.

Fasting can be self-directed or directed by God. For example, a person might choose to fast for a particular breakthrough. Isaiah informs us that he was instructed to pray.

> Cry aloud, spare not, lift up thy voice like a trumpet, and shew my people their transgression, and the house of Jacob their sins.

> Yet they seek me daily, and delight to know my ways, as a nation that did righteousness, and forsook not the ordinance of their God: they ask of me the ordinances of justice; they take delight in approaching to God (Isaiah 58:1,2).

After instructing Isaiah to fast, God revealed to him the benefits of fasting.

> Then shall thy light break forth as the morning, and thine health shall spring forth speedily: and thy righteousness shall go before thee; the glory of the Lord shall be thy reward.

> Then shalt thou call, and the Lord shall answer; thou shalt cry, and he shall say, Here I am. If thou take away from the midst of thee the yoke, the putting forth of the finger, and speaking vanity;

> And if thou draw out thy soul to the hungry, and satisfy the afflicted soul; then shall thy light rise in obscurity, and thy darkness be as the noonday:

> And the Lord shall guide thee continually, and satisfy thy soul in drought, and make fat thy bones: and thou shalt be like a watered garden, and like a spring of water, whose waters fail not.

And they that shall be of thee shall build the old waste places: thou shalt raise up the foundations of many generations; and thou shalt be called, The repairer of the breach, The restorer of paths to dwell in (Isaiah 58:8-12).

These tremendous blessings are available to any believer who obeys God in fasting. Those called to prophetic ministry, however, especially need to hear God's voice and be led by His Spirit. That's why prayer and fasting are a powerful combination in the prophet's life and ministry.

Chapter 6

The Gift of Prophecy

The apostle Paul gave prerequisites for ministry for those endowed with special gifts. Paul told us that the believer must walk in humility and he or she must not think themselves higher than others.

> Having then gifts differing according to the grace that is given to us, whether prophecy, let us prophesy according to the proportion of faith;
>
> Or ministry, let us wait on our ministering: or he that teacheth, on teaching;
>
> Or he that exhorteth, on exhortation: he that giveth, let him do it with simplicity; he that ruleth, with diligence; he that sheweth mercy, with cheerfulness (Romans 12:6-8).

Some people have the gift of prophecy. Others may have the ability to teach and bring forth illumination from the Scripture.

The simple gift of prophecy is an operation of the Holy Spirit; the individual receives a direct word from

God by His Spirit. The word usually builds faith and often brings comfort. This gift of God is exercised under the auspices of the Holy Spirit. Its primary function is to undergird the church for its task in ministry.

The gift is basically a function in the church administration that makes known the will of God to the local Body.

Many people make the mistake of confusing the ministry of the prophet and the gift of prophecy. The two are not the same.

The prophet is called by God to exercise a ministry to the entire church. His is a calling, a life-style, an ever-present activity.

The gift of prophecy is only exercised within the local church. Paul tells us that all may prophesy. He also points out in other epistles, however, that only some are called as prophets. The prophet's message brings direction. The gift of prophecy usually will not be directive in nature. Anyone can prophesy. But only those specially called, prepared, and equipped can stand in the office of the prophet.

Chapter 7

How to Judge Prophecy

Prophets do not operate in a vacuum; nor is the word of the Lord they utter beyond scrutiny. In fact, the apostle Paul actually encourages that the prophet's message be judged. "Let the prophets speak two or three, and let the other judge" (1 Corinthians 14:29).

The prophetic word should be weighed. Prophecies that are good should be retained; those contrary to the written Word of God should be rejected.

Every prophetic word needs to be judged by the prophet in the local church. This is to protect individuals from erroneous messages that could ruin their lives or detour them from the road God has called them to walk.

It is difficult for some people to differentiate between true and false prophets. Both will speak in the name of the Lord, but that does not mean they both have been given authority to speak. Scripture provides three criteria for proving whether a prophet is sent — or whether he went by his own directive.

The first test was the prophet's loyalty. Any prophet who worshiped other gods or walked in idolatry was not qualified to represent Jehovah.

> If there arise among you a prophet, or a dreamer of dreams, and giveth thee a sign or a wonder, and the sign or the wonder come to pass, whereof he spake unto thee, saying, Let us go after other gods, which thou hast not known, and let us serve them; Thou shalt not hearken unto the words of that prophet, or that dreamer of dreams: for the Lord your God proveth you, to know whether ye love the Lord your God with all your heart and with all your soul.

> Ye shall walk after the Lord your God, and fear him, and keep his commandments, and obey his voice, and ye shall serve him, and cleave unto him. And that prophet, or that dreamer of dreams, shall be put to death; because he hath spoken to turn you away from the Lord your God, which brought you out of the land of Egypt, and redeemed you out of the house of bondage, to thrust thee out of the way which the Lord thy God commanded thee to walk in. So shalt thou put the evil away from the midst of thee (Deuteronomy 13:1-5).

The second test to determine whether a prophet is true or false is to examine the character of the prophet. Isaiah notes that the false prophets were drunken and confused. "But they also have erred through wine, and through strong drink . . ." (Isaiah 28:7).

The third test is that true prophets do not prophesy what people want them to say.

And all the prophets prophesied so, saying, Go up to Ramoth-gilead, and prosper: for the Lord shall deliver it into the king's hand (1 Kings 22:12).

If God does not give a true prophet of God a word, he will be silent — no matter what pressure is exerted or reward is promised. A false prophet, however, will begin to conjure up visions and prophecies of his own. Jeremiah gives us clarity about these types of prophets.

The prophet that hath a dream, let him tell a dream, and he that hath my word, let him speak my word faithfully. What is the chaff to the wheat? saith the Lord.

Is not my word like as a fire? saith the Lord; and like a hammer that breaketh the rock in pieces?

Therefore, behold, I am against the prophets, saith the Lord, that steal my words every one from his neighbor.

Behold I am against the prophets, saith the Lord, that use their tongues, and say, He saith (Jeremiah 23:28-31).

True prophets will see a word that other men cannot see. Yet they speak words that other men can hear. When he speaks, the prophet commands attention. He often comes upon difficult, perplexing, disappointing, and sometimes dangerous situations.

Consistency in speech must be a building block in the prophetic foundation. The prophetic word was authenticated by its own inherent worth and weight, rather than by signs and by the personal power of the men who spoke it.

Almighty God upholds His prophetic word and acts powerfully to fulfill it. That's why prophecy often threatened those who held power in ecclesiastical, political, and economical arenas. God uses prophecy to remind us of His coming kingdom. We would be wise to align ourselves with His eternal plans and purposes.

Chapter 8

The Spirit of Prophecy

Anyone can prophesy as the Spirit of the Lord leads them. The spirit of prophecy is released to reveal the heart and mind of God. As God unveils His willingness to move in our lives, those present can receive ministry.

The spirit of prophecy is released when there is not a prophet in a particular church or region. It empowers a person to speak for God in the absence of the prophet. In many churches, the spirit of prophecy comes upon the mothers, missionaries, and evangelists.

The spirit of prophecy does not always bring interpretation or a word for prophecy. It may bring a word of knowledge or a word of wisdom. You may have to interpret as the Spirit of God uses you. Determine if you are giving an individual a word of knowledge or a word of wisdom. Or are you prophesying to them?

Prophecy is foretelling. It brings a taste, or foretelling, of one's future; what God is saying of things to come. A word of knowledge gives immediate understanding about situations. A word of wisdom provides supernatural ability and direct revelation to receive the wisdom of God. The term is derived from the Greek word *sophia,* which is wisdom.

The spirit of prophecy brings forth realignment. It provides insight into what God wants a person to do. Among other things, it brings structure, direction, establishment, foundation and articulation of what you need to receive. Prophecy may cover a variety of areas.

The spirit of prophecy is subject to the person who prophesies. The spirit of prophecy is not unseemly, or out of control. Not everyone who moves in the spirit of prophecy will be accurate for various reasons, including wrong motives.

One of the ways Jesus testifies is by the spirit of prophecy.

And I fell at his feet to worship him. And he said unto me, See thou do it not: I am thy fellowservant, and of thy brethren that have the testimony of Jesus: worship God: for the testimony of Jesus is the spirit of prophecy (Revelation 19:10).

Why does the angel tell John that he has the testimony of Jesus? Is he talking about His death, burial, and resurrection? No. The angel said, "for the testimony of Jesus is the spirit of prophecy." Jesus' life is a living prophecy.

The spirit of prophecy is a tremendous gift to the Body of Christ because it is the testimony of Jesus Christ Himself. The testimony comes through the prophetic interpretations of what has been heard and seen.

Wealth Wrapped in a Word

Prophecy is like gold dust: where there is little, it seems like it is not enough. It is possible to accumulate enough, however, to build a brick. The brick represents wealth. Like the gold brick, a prophecy represents accumulated wealth. This is why the enemy comes to rob you of that wealth.

Faith must be present for the spirit of prophecy to operate. Believers can only prophesy according to their faith. Many people say they are prophets, but they do not have much faith. We all have been given a "measure of faith" (Romans 12:3), but we are not all on the same level of faith. Faith grows when used. Mature faith will yield to the spirit of prophecy. A yielded vessel will be able to interpret what is seen.

We can prophesy because God reveals hidden things. The person prophesying will see a photograph, vision, or snapshot of something. "I see bands wrapped around your hands . . ." The image that is seen could represent something that is spiritual, physical, or emotional.

When the spirit of prophecy comes upon a person, he or she will experience the anointing of the Lord. They may even feel His presence.

The person with the spirit of prophecy can be denied entry into its uses, however, based on their motives. They might sincerely want to help a person with a personal problem, but no word comes from the Lord. Yet the troubled friend might continue to ask, "Do you see God doing anything about this?" If the person with the spirit of prophecy continues to look within for a word, Satan will give him or her a lying spirit.

One of the ministry errors of the spirit of prophecy is the person who begins to operate out of a selfish will. Some people stretch out and become overconfident in themselves because the spirit of prophecy is operating in their lives.

While we should covet prophesying (1 Corinthians 14:1), beware how you handle this gift. You could lead someone into error. You could be completely off. Stay on course, and speak only when the Spirit speaks.

Divine Direction

The spirit of prophecy brings direction. God will sometimes speak to single men and women regarding marriage. Women who are devoted to God often receive unexpected prophecies as they focus on serving Him.

People often desire prophecies about their financial situations or business ventures. Again, those with the spirit of prophecy should be careful that they speak only the oracles of God. A prophet is often used to help steer people to the right careers or investments. Examine the Scriptures concerning finances. Properly applying kingdom principles will enable anyone to handle their finances properly and to prosper.

> And thou shalt go down before me to Gilgal; and, behold, I will come down unto thee, to offer burnt offerings, and to sacrifice sacrifices of peace offerings; seven days shalt thou tarry, till I come to thee and shew thee what thou shalt do.

> And it was so, that when he had turned his back to go from Samuel, God gave him another heart: and all those signs came to pass that day (1 Samuel 10:8,9).

Samuel gave Saul divine direction — insight into God's plan for him. Prophets — not apostles, teachers, pastors, nor evangelists — have the only gift in the Bible most like God. Prophecy is most like God because God is strictly prophetic. Everything that God speaks is prophetic.

God "calls things that be not as though they were." God also makes crooked things straight. Only God can do these things. Only God can speak peace in a storm and life among the dead. The prophet is used by God to speak the word of the Lord in these areas to bring the needed transformation and resurrection.

Prophets reverse situations. Isaiah both released and reversed death in King Hezekiah's life (Isaiah 38:1-8).

The office of the prophet is the most hated office in the Body of Christ. Prophets are often called to correct the mindset and actions of church leaders who may not be operating according to Scripture. He may "put his finger on" favoritism, buddy systems, and selfish motives. A prophet may walk in and decree, "This whole system is wrong. Thus saith the Lord . . ." In such instances, the prophet is immediately unpopular.

A prophet can also release the spirit of prophecy. The Spirit of the Lord empowers the prophet to do this. The Spirit of the Lord came upon Saul when he met a company of prophets. What happened? He began to prophesy.

> And when they came thither to the hill, behold, a company of prophets met him; and the Spirit of God came upon him, and he prophesied among them.
>
> And it came to pass, when all that knew him beforetime saw that, behold, he prophesied among the prophets, then the people said one to another, What is this that is come unto the son of Kish? Is Saul also among the prophets?
>
> And one of the same place answered and said, But who is their father? Therefore it became a proverb, Is Saul also among the prophets?
>
> And when he had made an end of prophesying, he came to the high place (1 Samuel 10:10-13).

God transferred the prophets' anointing to Saul. Why was this necessary? Saul had been freshly anointed as king. Saul received wisdom so that he would have prophetic insight; no leader can function effectively without it.

All government officials and politicians, including the president — as well as those who serve in special roles such as head of the Federal Reserve Bank — are seers. They see down the road where the economy is going. They have to see. Sight is valuable.

Whenever there is a strong prophetic covering, there will be a desire to prophesy and to flow.

> This charge I commit unto thee, son Timothy, according to the prophecies which went before on thee, that thou by them mightest war a good warfare (1 Timothy 1:18).

The apostle Paul uses two strong words to get his point across: "charge" and "commit." Timothy had to know that this was a point of surrender and obedience.

He had a charge to be committed to the prophecies that went before him. Even though circumstances may seem to contradict what God has spoken prophetically, it is essential to hold fast the prophetic word. Walk by it. Keep the charge.

Believers who do not have a vision of the future should consider the prophecies that went before them. Real prophetic impartation aligns you with your purpose. God will speak direction. The impartation will help the believer to master areas of slothfulness and procrastination that may have been difficult to conquer.

Caution: guard your tongue concerning unfulfilled prophecies. You may blaspheme by insinuating God is a liar because the prophetic word has yet to come to pass. God is merciful, but He will not deal lightly with a blasphemer.

In addition to a charge, the apostle Paul instructs Timothy to fight. A person must wage war according to the word of the Lord spoken into his or her life. Focus is the key. Disregard all circumstances and imaginations contrary to the prophecy. If God has shown the photograph, it will surely come to pass. Cherish the prophetic word. Pray it.

> Wherefore I put thee in remembrance that thou stir up the gift of God, which is in thee by the putting on of my hands (2 Timothy 1:6).

> Neglect not the gift that is in thee, which was given thee by prophecy, with the laying on of the hands of the presbytery (1 Timothy 4:14).

Timothy had a gift given by prophecy and the laying on of hands, but he also had to stir it up and use it. How? He had to develop a deep inner relationship with the Holy Ghost. The gift must be stirred until it begins rising and operating in a person's life.

God wants His children to be good stewards. We must become good managers of our lives before the prophetic word comes to pass. God is not going to give His gifts to wasters. Management is the key to abundant blessing.

> "For unto whomsoever much is given, of him shall be much required: and to whom men have committed much, of him they will ask the more" (Luke 12:48).

Chapter 9

Faith and Prophecy

Some prophecies have been shipwrecked because the recipients did not follow the prophecy. God may have given specific instructions — for example, "wait" — and the person did not follow the instructions. Other believers give up and do not hold fast to their faith.

> Holding faith, and a good conscience; which some having put away concerning faith have made shipwreck: (1 Timothy 1:19).

> Now faith is the substance of things hoped for, the evidence of things not seen (Hebrews 11:1).

> And now abideth faith, hope, charity, these three . . . (1 Corinthians 13:13).

Without faith it is impossible to please God. A doubting Thomas will never receive anything from God because he is double-minded. If you doubt the veracity of your prophecy, you will not embrace it. When the fulfillment is ready to come to pass, you will not open your door to the divine connection, correction, or intervention that God has prepared for you.

Failing to embrace prophecy may cause you to miss your season of visitation. To everything there is a purpose. If you miss the purpose, you will miss seeing the fulfillment of your prophecy. Even when you don't understand the prophetic word, embrace it! Run toward it. Ponder it in your heart, even though it is mysterious.

The prophetic ministry delves into the mysteries of God. The prophet speaks the oracles of God; the actual words of God. The only way a prophet can do this effectively is by faith. It takes faith to minister prophetically about situations, events, and people about which you know little or nothing.

Exercising faith is the only way the prophet can assure that he is pleasing God.

But without faith it impossible to please him: for he that cometh to God must believe that he is, and that he is a rewarder of them that diligently seek him (Hebrews 11:6).

The fulfillment of your prophecy can be considered a reward. Do you believe God can reward you by bringing your word to pass? If not, you will miss the blessing.

Faith and prophecy work hand in hand. Faith is the fuel that enables the man of God to reach deep within the prophetic. As faith increases, the prophet is able to descend deeper into the things of God.

The prophet must safeguard his faith from people who misunderstand or abuse the prophetic ministry. All faith must be challenged to prove that "If thou canst believe, all things are possible to him that believeth" (Mark 9:23). Each time faith is exercised, the results will be monumental. The prophet is both a man of faith and a faith builder. When he stands before someone to minister, faith is already working. Faith works to minister the word of the Lord and to build up the faith of the hearer.

> Having then gifts differing according to the grace that is given to us, whether prophecy, let us prophesy according to the proportion of faith (Romans 12:6).

As the prophet speaks he utters the revealed word. The prophet that prophesies in this manner will continue to flow in faith. Jude 1:20 provides a key: "But ye, beloved, building up yourselves on your most holy faith, praying in the Holy Ghost."

Like exercising the muscles of his physical body, the prophet must tone up his spiritual man. A good workout will not be complete without the prophet exercising his faith.

Maintaining a steadfast faith in God will help the prophet keep his sanity when he goes through unexpected dry places and storms of controversy. The prophet will victoriously weather such situations if he follows the apostle Jude's advice to consistently pray in the Holy Ghost.

Selected Bibliography

Grudem, Wayne. *The Gift of Prophecy in the New Testament Today.* (Eastborne, England: Kingsway Publications.)

Hill, Clifford. *Prophecy, Past and Present.* (Ann Arbor, Michigan: Servant Publications, 1989.)

Scott, R.B.Y. *The Relevance of the Prophets.* (New York: The MacMillan Company.)

Wood, Leon. *The Prophets of Israel.* (Grand Rapids, Michigan: Baker Book House.)

About the Author

Prophet Kervin J. Smith is the President of Kervin J. Smith Ministries, an international and interracial ministry that is penetrating many major inner cities of America.

Prophet Smith is a former financial consultant who has been given a mandate by God to present a clear prophetic insight to the Body of Christ. He has been featured on many talk shows, radio forums, and symposiums, as well as Trinity Broadcasting Network.

He is also the author of *Body Building: Getting the Church in Shape for God's Blessing.*

For more information contact:

Prophet Kervin J. Smith
Kervin J. Smith Ministries
P.O. Box 119
Short Hills, NJ 07078

get back on our feet. The cause of the fall is not as important as what we do while we're down. T.D. Jakes explains how – and Whom – to ask for help. In a struggle to regain your balance, this book is going to be your manual to recovery! Don't panic. This is just a test!

Becoming A Leader
by Myles Munroe

Many consider leadership to be no more than staying ahead of the pack, but that is a far cry from what leadership is. Leadership is deploying others to become as good as or better than you are. Within each of us lies the potential to be an effective leader. *Becoming A Leader* uncovers the secrets of dynamic leadership that will show you how to be a leader in your family, school, community, church and job. No matter where you are or what you do in life this book can help you to inevitably become a leader. Remember: it is never too late to become a leader. As in every tree there is a forest, so in every follower there is a leader.

The African Cultural Heritage Topical Bible

The African Cultural Heritage Topical Bible is a quick and convenient reference Bible. It has been designed for use in personal devotions as well as group Bible studies. It's the newest and most complete reference Bible designed to reveal the Black presence in the Bible and highlight the contributions and exploits of Blacks from the past to present. It's a great tool for students, clergy, teachers — practically anyone seeking to learn more about the Black presence in Scripture, but didn't know where to start.

The African Cultural Heritage Topical Bible contains:
• Over **395** easy to find **topics**
• **3,840 verses** that are systematically organized
• A comprehensive listing of Black Inventions
• Over **150 pages** of Christian Afrocentric articles on Blacks in the Bible, Contributions of Africa, African Foundations of Christianity, Culture, Identity, Leadership, and Racial Reconciliation written by Myles Munroe, Wayne Perryman, Dr. Leonard Lovett, Dr. Trevor L. Grizzle, James Giles, and Mensa Otabil.

Available in KJV and NIV versions

The God Factor
by James Giles

Is something missing in your life? Do you find yourself at the mercy of your circumstances? Is your self-esteem at an all-time low? Are your dreams only a faded memory? You could be missing the one element that could make the difference between success and failure, poverty and prosperity, and creativity and apathy. Knowing God supplies the creative genius you need to reach your potential and realize your dream. You'll be challenged as James Giles shows you how to tap into your God-given genius, take steps toward reaching your goal, pray big and get answers, eat right and stay healthy, prosper economically and personally, and leave a lasting legacy for your children.

Making the Most of Your Teenage Years
by David Burrows

Most teenagers live for today. Living only for today, however, can kill you. When teenagers have no plan for their future, they follow a plan that someone else devised. Unfortunately, this plan often leads them to drugs, sex, crime, jail, and an early death. How can you make the most of your teenage years? Discover who you really are – and how to plan for the three phases of your life. You can develop your skill, achieve your dreams, and still have fun.

Beyond the Rivers of Ethiopia
by Mensa Otabil

Beyond the Rivers of Ethiopia is a powerful and revealing look into God's purpose for the Black race. It gives scholastic yet simple answers to questions you have always had about the Black presence in the Bible. At the heart of this book is a challenge and call to the offspring of the Children of Africa, both on the continent and throughout the world, to come to grips with their true identity as they go *Beyond the Rivers of Ethiopia.*

Single Life
by Earl D. Johnson

A book that candidly addresses the spiritual and physical dimensions of the single life is finally here. *Single Life* shows the reader how to make their singleness a celebration rather than a burden. This positive approach to singles uses enlightening examples from Apostle Paul, himself a single, to beautifully portray the dynamic aspects of the single life by serving the Lord more effectively. The book gives fresh insight on practical issues such as coping with sexual desires, loneliness, and preparation for your future mate. Written in a lively style, the author admonishes singles to seek first the kingdom of God and rest assured in God's promise to supply their needs... including a life partner!